Dedicated to You.

This is a story about a fly named Freddy.
Who wanted to fly, but he just wasn't ready.
Maybe he could learn to fly if he had the right help.
He had a big family, but mostly kept to himself.
Even Henry could fly, and he was overweight.
His sister Susie could fly, and so could his cousin Kate.
He wanted to fly but decided to wait.
Even when he saw food he wanted on a plate.

He thought it was odd and really quite weird.
Even grandpa could fly, with his long fluffy beard.
Maybe it just wasn't his time, and he wasn't prepared.
But the truth was that Freddy was just scared.
He made excuses every time he would talk.
"I don't need to fly. I'll just use my legs to walk."
Sofia, Gerald, and Lenny were some of his friends.
"I never saw a fly that couldn't fly" the joke never ends.

Freddy couldn't resist joining in on the laughing.
He was embarrassed when his wings started flapping.
It really made it sad because he didn't like how they were acting.
They used to wonder why he didn't fly, but everyone stopped asking.
The others would fly around when it was time to play.
They did this all through the night and every single day.
When all the flies left Freddy would just stay.
"I'm okay" is all he would say.

Until one day, Freddy's dad whispered in his ear.

"I'm going to tell you something you really need to hear."

"No matter what happens, I'll always be near."

But I think it's time I help you conquer this fear."

Freddy started to tremble and shake and even tried to escape.

"Wait, I made you this cape!"

"Son, I promise that everything will be fine."
"You say that I am your hero, but really you're mine."
Freddy's dad held up the cape, and it glowed in the light.
He put it around Freddy's neck, and then tied it tight.
Just then, Freddy's friends flew by and gave him a wave.
Freddy made it up in his mind that he would be brave.

His dad sat there patiently and waited awhile.
Until Freddy looked back and gave him a smile.
Freddy flapped his wings and started off slow.
He lifted up a little bit and his courage started
to grow.
His wings went faster and became part of the
flow.
His cape shined bright with a nice golden glow.

He looked down at his dad as someone he would always admire.
Freddy told him to take a picture, and then he flew higher.
He realized flying was possible, even if it took several tries.
He caught up with Sofia, Gerald, Lenny, and the rest of the flies.
They were so happy for Freddy that they didn't know what to say.
They complimented Freddy's cape and told him it was perfect to play.
They flew around all day and stayed in the air for hours.
Freddy was so thankful that his cape gave him flying superpowers.
It was his favorite color and was nice and soft.
Even when he slept, Freddy didn't take it off.

One day, Freddy and his friends were playing and flying around.
Freddy's cape came untied and slowly fell to the ground.
Freddy zoomed all over and kept flying about.
Until Lenny got his attention and gave him a shout.
"Freddy, your cape came off and you never even noticed."
Freddy looked at his cape on the ground and just stayed focused.
He kept flapping his wings and then he just stared.
Freddy wasn't wearing his magic cape, but no longer cared.

Freddy wanted to talk to his dad and tell him the surprise.

His dad already knew from the look in his eyes.

"Dad, do you see something about me that looks a little different?"

Freddy's father already knew in an instant.

"I was flying so fast that I don't even know what happened."

"The cape fell off, but I kept my wings flapping."

Freddy's dad already knew how it was done.

This made him a little prouder of his son.

Freddy was so excited that he didn't know what to do.

On that day, Freddy and his dad's connection grew.

Freddy had many questions and asked his father a few.

Freddy's father gave him the answer for two.

The last question was something Freddy possibly knew.

"Dad, did the cape really give me superpowers? Is that really true?"

Freddy's dad looked at him with a smile and said...

"The power was already in YOU."